Inspiration.

How to Unlock Your Passion and Creativity

Josh Floyd

INSPIRATION

Text by Katherine Bassford

An Hachette UK Company
www.hachette.co.uk

Vie Books, an imprint of Summersdale Publishers Ltd
Part of Octopus Publishing Group Limited
Carmelite House
50 Victoria Embankment
LONDON
EC4Y 0DZ
UK

www.summersdale.com

Printed and bound in the Czech Republic

ISBN: 978-1-78783-263-3

Substantial discounts on bulk quantities of Summersdale books are available to corporations, professional associations and other organizations. For details contact general enquiries: telephone: +44 (0) 1243 771107 or email: enquiries@summersdale.com.

Introduction

We all want to feel joy, passion and purpose in our lives, but it can be hard to stay motivated and enthusiastic when faced with the demands of everyday life. Thankfully, there is inspiration all around us, whether you find it while sleeping under the stars, by spending time with optimistic people, or in reviving a long-lost ambition. New experiences can open the floodgates to fresh perspectives and ideas, so if you're feeling stuck or uninspired, dip into this book and try something new today. These motivating quotes and simple tips are designed to help you tap into your creativity, reignite your passion and open your eyes to exciting new possibilities.

BREAK FROM THE ORDINARY

If you're stuck in the same old routine, it's time to try something new. Spend a day (or at least a few hours) purposely departing from your normal routine: tune in to a different radio station, take a new route to work, visit an unusual shop or say "hi" to a neighbour you don't normally talk to. Take every opportunity to experience your world in brand new ways. By widening your perspective, you'll expose yourself to new ideas and inspirations.

Catch the trade winds in your sails. Explore. Dream. Discover.

H. Jackson Brown Jr

Write a Bucket List

It's easy to get caught up in a flurry of day-to-day activities and forget what you really want from life. A "bucket list" is a list of all the goals and dreams you want to achieve in your lifetime, and can be a great way of reminding you of what's really important. To create your list, think of all the things you want to do, see, feel and experience. Keep going until you have at least 50 items on your list. If you find yourself stuck, you may be mentally limiting yourself.

Let yourself go – what would you do if you had unlimited time, money and resources? What have you always wanted to do but not yet done? Items on your list may be "big", such as travelling around the world, or "small", such as seeing your favourite band play live. Once you've written your list, start ticking off the goals you achieve and add any new ones that come to mind. Writing a bucket list should encourage you to live life to the full.

ALL LIFE IS AN
EXPERIMENT. THE MORE
EXPERIMENTS YOU
MAKE, THE BETTER.

Ralph Waldo Emerson

Happiness is a way of travel, not a destination.

Roy M. Goodman

Say Yes

If you're feeling uninspired, doing something spontaneous may not be the most obvious solution. However, doing something fun or unusual may be just what you need to lift your spirits. A good way to practise this is to start saying "yes" to things. If you're invited to a party that you wouldn't normally attend, say "yes" and make yourself go. If you walk past a poster advertising a dance or photography class you've always secretly wanted to try, sign up the second you get home. By saying "yes" to possibilities that are placed before you, you'll open your world to new people, places and experiences. This will probably entail stepping out of your comfort zone, but the benefits include more spontaneity, excitement and adventure. Try saying "yes" to life for an hour, a day or a month and see what happens.

Look on every exit
as being an entrance
somewhere else.

Tom Stoppard

SEE THE SUNRISE

Have you ever taken the time to sit and watch a sunrise? This wonder of nature can fill you with awe and reverence. Check the weather, pick a clear day and find a beautiful spot. The sun rises in the east and sets in the west, so make sure you have a clear view. Arrive in plenty of time, wrap up warm, and enjoy. You won't need to go back to bed afterward – you'll be inspired and ready to take on the day.

CREATE
A BUZZ

One of the biggest challenges with meeting goals is finding the motivation to keep going. This can feel like an uphill struggle at times, but there are simple tricks that can help you generate energy and excitement to propel you toward your dream. Whether you dream of entering a triathlon or starting a new business, seek inspiration from others. Talk to your partner about your idea or share your thoughts with a supportive friend. Chat to like-minded people via local clubs or online forums. Imagine what it would feel like to achieve your ambition, and visualize yourself succeeding. Motivation is not a constant thing – it will come and go – but by surrounding yourself with positive people and images, you'll generate the buzz and excitement that will keep you moving toward your goal.

The foolish man seeks happiness in the distance; the wise grows it under his feet.

James Oppenheim

Be the calm centre in the raging flow of life.

Leo Babauta

Secret Desires

Is there something you've secretly always wanted to try? Many of us have heartfelt desires we have buried deep inside us. Maybe you've always wanted to learn to dance, play the drums or go rock climbing? Think of something you've always longed to do and find a way to experience it in some way. Booking a lesson or taster session may mean stepping out of your comfort zone for a while, but it will boost your confidence, light up your soul and fill you with a sense of accomplishment. No matter how things turn out, you'll know you had the courage to try something new. You'll realize the only thing holding you back is your thinking – and with this thought, an exciting new world will start to open up to you.

YOUR MIND IS YOUR
INSTRUMENT. LEARN
TO BE ITS MASTER AND
NOT ITS SLAVE.

Remez Sasson

DOODLE POWER

Reconnect with your inner child and start doodling. Experts say doodling is a quick and effective way to switch off your thinking and unleash your creativity. Whatever you draw – whether you create shapes, patterns or letters – a doodle is not supposed to be a work of art, so you can relax and just have fun expressing yourself. Place a pad of paper and some pens on your desk or beside your bed, so that you can pick up a pen and let your mind wander whenever you feel the urge.

TRY TO BE LIKE THE TURTLE – AT EASE IN YOUR OWN SHELL.

BILL COPELAND

Everything you do can be done better from a place of relaxation.

Stephen C. Paul

CAPTURING BEAUTY

Take a camera outside and photograph anything that looks beautiful to you. This could be a stunning view or a piece of architecture, or it could be something less obvious such as a colourful fabric, the texture of rust, or an old door. By actively looking for beautiful things, you'll train your brain to notice feel-good people, places and objects, and you'll start to see more of the beauty that surrounds you.

**Energy and persistence
conquer all things.**

Benjamin Franklin

Express Yourself

Being creative is a great way to express your thoughts, feelings and ideas. It can help you make sense of your experiences and the world around you. Try expressing yourself creatively in a way you've never done before, such as drawing, singing or photography. There are adult education classes in all sorts of subjects, but if you'd rather not commit to a class, you could get a "how to" book from the library, watch an instructional video online, or take up a creative hobby you can learn by yourself at home, such as painting. Whatever you do, choose something that sounds like fun. Remember, anyone can be creative. No matter the outcome, if you're embracing this side of your personality, you're always winning. Experimenting with new or unusual creative outlets can lead to new thoughts and unexpected breakthroughs. At the very least, you'll have a blast.

WITH THE NEW DAY
COMES NEW STRENGTH
AND NEW THOUGHTS.

Eleanor Roosevelt

It does not matter how slowly you go as long as you do not stop.

Confucius

A BIRTHDAY EVERY DAY!

Our birthday is often one of the most memorable days of the year, whether we opt for a meal in a restaurant, a party at home, or a day out with family or friends. Birthdays are a chance to celebrate life, to feel special and to spend quality time with loved ones. So why wait another 364 days to enjoy life to the fullest? Why not celebrate each day with the magic of a birthday? Treat yourself to something nice – book a massage or buy yourself a gift, for example. Or turn the tables and treat someone else: buy a big helium balloon for a friend or bake them a cake for no reason other than to show your appreciation. It needn't cost a lot of money: simply making time to be with loved ones or inviting a friend over for a meal can be just as special. Live each day as if it's your birthday and you'll experience a year full of memorable days.

It's more fun
to be the painter
than the paint.

George Clooney

WATCH TED

If you're in need of inspiration, head to www.ted.com. TED is a non-profit organization devoted to spreading ideas in the form of short, powerful talks by the world's most inspired thinkers. On the TED website you'll discover talks on every conceivable topic, from science to art to global issues. You can browse the library of more than 2,000 talks and engage with a community of like-minded curious souls on their TED Conversations platform.

The prerequisite for me is to keep my well of ideas full. This means living as full and varied a life as possible.

Michael Morpurgo

Throw caution to the wind and just do it.

Carrie Underwood

Write a Love List

It's easy to take things for granted in life. A simple way to amplify your feeling of gratitude and abundance is to write a "Love List". Sit down with a pen and paper and make a list of everything that you are passionate about. Don't limit yourself. This is about listing all the things you love, not what other people think. Include all the things, people, places and concepts that bring you joy and make your heart sing. These items can be as big or small as you like. Write your list in a special notebook and review it regularly. It's easy to be bogged down by our To Do lists and endless obligations. Writing a Love List will help reconnect you with the myriad things that make your life happier – from being greeted in the morning by your dog to walking outside in the sunshine.

AS SOON AS YOU
START TO PURSUE
A DREAM, YOUR
LIFE WAKES UP
AND EVERYTHING
HAS MEANING.

BARBARA SHER

**Your chances
of success in
any undertaking
can always be
measured by your
belief in yourself.**

Robert Collier

Choose a New Habit

On average, it takes around two months before a new behaviour becomes a habit. Make today the day you embrace a new healthy habit that has the power to change your life for the better. You could commit to a weekly yoga class or meditate for five minutes every night. Whatever you choose, make sure it's something doable. Setting big goals can feel daunting, so taking baby steps greatly increases your odds of success. If your goal is to run or meditate for an hour a day, for example, there will probably be many days when you don't run or meditate at all. However, if you make your goal walking around the block or one minute of mindful breathing, you can certainly accomplish that. As time goes by, you will feel proud that you've honoured your commitment to yourself. And crucially, you will have created a new neural pathway in your brain that turns your daily activity into a habit.

Angels can fly
because they can take
themselves lightly.

G. K. Chesterton

NEW HORIZONS

Travelling is a great way to broaden your mind and get out of your comfort zone. It exposes you to new cultures and all sorts of people you would never normally encounter. Admittedly, we can't all afford to take a year out to travel the world, but we can holiday in new or unusual places and plan more weekend getaways. Seek out new horizons and see how it energizes your mind, body and spirit.

SEE AND BELIEVE

Our minds respond strongly to visual stimulation. Surrounding yourself with images of your goals and ideal life can stimulate your emotions and fill you with the enthusiasm you need to take steps toward your dreams. A simple way to do this is to create a "Vision Board" of positive words and pictures that symbolize the experiences, feelings and possessions you want to attract into your life. Your "board" could be a notice board, folder, scrapbook or online pinboard. The important thing is that you fill it with images and words that excite and inspire you, such as photos, pictures from magazines and motivational quotes. Your Vision Board is an image of the future, a representation of what you are working toward. Place it somewhere you can see it every day (or set it as your homepage when you open an internet browser) and regularly visualize, affirm and believe in your goals. Have fun with the process and cherish your Vision Board – it can be a powerful catalyst in the creation of your dreams.

SOMETIMES YOU NEED
TO TAKE A DEPARTURE
FROM WHAT YOU DO
TO SOMETHING THAT'S
SLIGHTLY DIFFERENT
IN ORDER TO GET
INSPIRATION.

Tori Amos

**When you reach the end
of your rope, tie a knot
in it and hang on.**

Anonymous

Wonderful Workspaces

Your workspace directly affects your productivity and creativity. Take a look around your office or home desk space. Does it inspire you and reflect who you are, or is it dull and boring? Start to notice where and when you are most creative. Do you need peace and quiet, or does chatter or music help you? Do you work best when there are no visual distractions, or do you need colour and pattern to inspire you? While it may be impractical to transform an office, you might be able to make small tweaks to your surroundings, such as hanging your favourite art or quote on the wall, moving your desk nearer to the window or placing a plant nearby. It can be hard to produce innovative work when your subconscious is saying, "I can't work here." An environment that suits your needs and personality can help you feel naturally inspired and motivated.

Aerodynamically, the bumblebee shouldn't be able to fly, but the bumblebee doesn't know so it goes flying anyway.

Mary Kay Ash

Change your thoughts and you change the world.

Norman Vincent Peale

EXERCISE YOUR BRAIN

Studies show that exercise stimulates the growth of new neurons in the brain. It can also boost your creativity and help you come up with new solutions to problems. Try to engage in regular physical activity such as walking, running, cycling, swimming or yoga. Aim to do something most days of the week, even if it's simply going for a brisk walk in your lunch hour. Getting in motion will boost your productivity and encourage new ideas and thought patterns.

THE MAIN THING IS
TO BE MOVED, TO
LOVE, TO HOPE, TO
TREMBLE, TO LIVE.

Auguste Rodin

Tap into Your Subconscious

Trying to force yourself to be constantly productive and creative can be harmful to your creativity. Studies show our most creative thoughts occur when we alternate between periods of intense, focused work and rest and relaxation. This is because when our minds are calm and uncluttered we are able to tap into our subconscious, which is believed to be vastly more powerful than our conscious mind. Take advantage of this by building periods of rest into your day. After you've spent some time working on a problem, take a break from what you're doing and go for a walk, meditate, or stand up and stretch. Avoid watching TV or doing any activity that saturates your mind with information during this break, and instead engage in a non-stressful, physical task such as gardening, cooking or washing the dishes, as your subconscious mind works best when your conscious mind is pleasantly occupied.

IF YOU CAN FIND A PATH WITH NO OBSTACLES, IT PROBABLY DOESN'T LEAD ANYWHERE.

FRANK A. CLARK

Optimism is the faith that leads to achievement.

———————————————

Helen Keller

CONNECTING THE DOTS

Steve Jobs talked about "connecting the dots" in his famous Stanford commencement speech – the road ahead may seem unclear, but you can't connect the dots of your life looking forward; you can only connect them when you're looking back. In his speech he recalled how he dropped out of college and took a class in calligraphy, thinking it would have no practical application in his life whatsoever. Ten years later, he used the ideas he learned in his calligraphy class to help design the first Macintosh computer, complete with beautiful typefaces. If he had never dropped out of college he would never have taken the calligraphy class and personal computers might be vastly different today. It can be helpful to remind yourself of this story when you're struggling to reach a goal. Have faith in yourself and follow your heart, curiosity and intuition. Trust that the dots in your life will somehow connect and you will ultimately realize your dreams.

REMAIN CALM, SERENE, ALWAYS IN COMMAND OF YOURSELF. YOU WILL THEN FIND OUT HOW EASY IT IS TO GET ALONG.

Paramahansa Yogananda

Better than a thousand hollow words, is one word that brings peace.

Buddha

INDULGE IN A CLASSIC

"Classic" books are called that for a reason – they have stood the test of time and are loved by readers around the world. Examples include *Pride and Prejudice* by Jane Austen and *On the Road* by Jack Kerouac. Google "classic books" and pick one to read this week. You'll definitely gain something from the experience. Whether it's pure pleasure or deep insight, the classics can enrich you in unexpected ways.

Tension is who
you think you should
be. Relaxation is
who you are.

Chinese proverb

What If?

If you're feeling stuck, a simple way to open yourself up to possibilities is to ask the question "What if?" The words we use can influence how our brains work, so using positive statements and open questions, such as "I can solve this", "There's always a way" and "What if?", can encourage lateral thinking and exploration. In contrast, negative or closed-ended statements, such as "I don't know" or "I can't", can restrict your thinking and creativity.

making it more likely that you'll remain stuck. The next time you need to come up with a solution to a problem, try using an open-ended question such as "What if there was a better solution to this?" Repeating this to yourself, like a creative mantra, will help your subconscious come up with answers. Try not to force a solution to appear. Relax and let inspirations and solutions emerge naturally and spontaneously.

The key to everything is patience. You get the chicken by hatching the egg, not by smashing it.

Arnold H. Glasow

Every artist was first an amateur.

Ralph Waldo Emerson

SLEEP UNDER THE STARS

Camping is a great way to reconnect with nature and leave your worries behind. Turn the TV off, leave your tablet at home and head out into the countryside or to a campsite. Take some food and a camping stove, or make your own campfire and cook dinner over an open flame. For a real sense of adventure, try sleeping under the stars in your sleeping bag, with a bivouac bag if it's cold.

DREAM LOFTY
DREAMS, AND AS
YOU DREAM, SO YOU
SHALL BECOME.

James Allen

HE IS A WISE MAN
WHO DOES NOT
GRIEVE FOR THE THINGS
WHICH HE HAS NOT,
BUT REJOICES FOR
THOSE WHICH HE HAS.

Epictetus

ONLINE INSPIRATION

There's a huge community of creative people on the internet all eager to discuss ideas and offer motivation and support. Blogs, forums and websites such as Pinterest, Twitter and Flickr allow you to follow and discuss the work of artists and innovators. Whether the medium is paint, photography, art or architecture, other people's artistic endeavours can jump-start your own creativity. And you might also meet a potential collaborator for your next creative venture.

A Day of Randomness

Do you find it difficult to make up your mind about trivial things, such as which restaurant to go to or which film to see? The next time you're faced with a small choice, instead of agonizing for hours, flip a coin and go with the answer you're given. This will free up your thinking and lead to some unexpected outcomes.

Perhaps you turn left instead of right when riding your bike in a city and discover an exciting new café or shop, or you read a sci-fi book you wouldn't normally read and realize you love the genre. Randomness can also be a useful time-saving tool. Try closing your eyes in a restaurant and picking an item from the menu with your finger, then you can get back to chatting with your friends. Dedicate a day or a weekend to making random choices. It will get you in the habit of making decisions more quickly, and it may lead to one or two adventures.

YOU CAN'T USE UP
CREATIVITY. THE
MORE YOU USE, THE
MORE YOU HAVE.

MAYA ANGELOU

No star is ever lost we once have seen, We always may be what we might have been.

Adelaide Anne Procter

A JOURNEY OF A
THOUSAND MILES
BEGINS WITH A
SINGLE STEP.

Lao Tzu

FAMILY ROOTS

Uncovering your ancestors' stories can be a fascinating process which can help you understand who you are and how you fit into the bigger world around you. Do you know what your ancestors were like and what experiences they lived through? Perhaps you're related to someone famous, or someone who lived through a historic event. Look up your family tree and see what you can discover. There are several online resources that can help you with this.

PEOPLE OFTEN SAY
THAT MOTIVATION
DOESN'T LAST.
WELL, NEITHER
DOES BATHING
– THAT'S WHY WE
RECOMMEND
IT DAILY.

Zig Ziglar

I have found that if you love life, life will love you back.

Arthur Rubinstein

▌▌▌ IT'S NEVER TOO LATE

Ask your parents to tell you what you were like as a child. What did you most enjoy doing? Often the things that mattered to us back then are signposts of buried dreams or activities that can fill our days with more joy. Did you used to sing at the top of your lungs, love climbing trees, or spend hours illustrating and writing stories? Can you remember your childhood dreams? Did you long to own a puppy, become an athlete, or explore the Amazon rainforest? See if you can identify one or two things you used to love or longed to do, and then aim to experience them now in some small way. Perhaps you could offer to walk your neighbour's dog, sign up for an exercise class, or book an adventure holiday for your next trip? Whatever your secret ambition, it's never too late to reconnect with an old dream.

Release opinions, free yourself from views. Be open to mystery.

Jack Kornfield

TAKE YOURSELF ON A DATE

Taking yourself out on a "date" can be a refreshing and liberating experience. You could sit in a café with a cappuccino, take a blanket and a book to the park, or enjoy a film at the cinema. Quality time alone is good for the soul and self-confidence. It can nurture your playfulness and fire up your imagination, as you revel in your own company.

YOU ARE NEVER TOO
OLD TO SET ANOTHER
GOAL OR TO DREAM
A NEW DREAM.

Les Brown

BE PREPARED

You never know when inspiration will strike. Carry a notebook with you at all times so you can jot down your thoughts and ideas. You can use your notebook to record funny conversations you overhear and inspiring quotes you come across, or even sketch the café or bar that you're in. Leaf through your notebook whenever you're stuck for creative ideas.

Look at everything as though you were seeing it for the first or last time.

Betty Smith

Life begins at the end of your comfort zone.

Neale Donald Walsch

WATCH YOUR WORDS

We frequently use words that undermine or sabotage us. Watch how often you use words such as "should", "can't", "impossible" and "hate". Try to omit these words from your vocabulary and use more encouraging words as you go about your day, such as "choose", "yes" and "love". Words have power. They shape our thoughts and influence our actions. Focus on positive words that fill you with hope and confidence and watch your self-belief start to soar.

A HAPPY LIFE CONSISTS NOT IN THE ABSENCE, BUT IN THE MASTERY OF HARDSHIPS.

HELEN KELLER

If you ask me what I came into this life to do, I will tell you: I came to live out loud.

Émile Zola

When life looks
like it's falling apart,
it may just be
falling in place.

Beverly Solomon

FACE FORWARD

You can't start the next chapter of your life if you keep re-reading the last one. Whatever has happened in the past, leave it behind you and move on. Don't allow past pains and regrets to affect the present moment and hold you back. Each day is a chance to start afresh and put your best foot forward, so focus on where you're going.

NEVER UNDERESTIMATE THE POWER OF PASSION.

Eve Sawyer

The Wonder of Nature

We live on a beautiful planet, full of astounding plants and animals, and yet most of us see a tiny fraction of the wonders around us. Research has shown that being in nature can help aid concentration and productivity, relieve stress and depression and give us an all-round sense of well-being, and there are lots of ways to welcome nature into your life. Fill your home with flowers, tend an allotment and go for bracing walks in the countryside. Be like a kid again – jump in puddles kick up leaves and forage for unusual feathers and stones. Experience the beauty of the world's oceans, forests and jungles by watching nature documentaries (even "faking it" can give you the same benefits as the real thing). Don't forget to appreciate the plants, animals and scenery of your neighbourhood too. There is beauty all around us if we pause long enough to look. Take every opportunity to connect with nature and let it calm, strengthen and inspire you.

I CAN'T CHANGE
THE DIRECTION OF
THE WIND, BUT I CAN
ADJUST MY SAILS TO
ALWAYS REACH MY
DESTINATION.

Jimmy Dean

The man who removes a mountain begins by carrying away small stones.

Confucius

Dream Big

Achieving our goals requires
energy and enthusiasm.
Often the only difference
between those who
succeed and those who fail
is that the successful carry
on when the unsuccessful
give up. A great way to keep
your motivation flowing is
to visualize your success
in great detail. Close your
eyes and imagine how your
dream outcome will look,

feel, smell, taste and sound. Utilize all your senses to make the experience as vivid and real as possible. Imagine where you are when you are successful. What do your surroundings look like? Who are you with? What are you wearing? How do you feel? Form as clear a mental picture as possible and repeat this process for at least a few minutes every day. Repetition is crucial. Motivation isn't something that stays with us forever; it needs to be constantly refreshed. Daily visualization is a powerful technique that can keep your motivation levels high over a long period of time.

For myself I am an optimist – it does not seem to be much use being anything else.

Winston Churchill

Life shrinks or expands according to one's courage.

Anaïs Nin

WRITE
A NOTE

In this age of email and text, handwritten notes are a long-lost art form, yet we all appreciate a personally written letter or card. They bring a warmth and pleasure to our world that digital communication can't replicate. Think of someone you haven't been in touch with for a while, or someone you would like to thank, and write them a handwritten note. Take some time to consider what sort of card, paper or pen would be most fitting. Whether you use a fountain pen on luxury paper, or colourful ink in a quirky card, putting pen to paper will show someone how much you care in a way that sending an email or a text never could. You'll benefit greatly too – expressing love and gratitude can help you experience better health and life satisfaction.

BE A TOURIST

It's easy to take your home town for granted. Are your eyes open to all the possibilities right on your doorstep? Take some time to explore your own town or city as if you were a newcomer to the area. Visit all the popular tourist sites and attractions. Check out the museums, parks, cafés and art galleries you've never been to before. Start to see your home town with fresh eyes – and don't forget your camera!

Art happens all the time, everywhere. All we have to do is to keep our minds open.

Jacek Tylicki

On the Move

Children don't worry about "exercise" or "fitness" but they are constantly moving. They run, climb, squat, crawl, jump and cartwheel. As adults, we've forgotten these natural movements and the increased strength, flexibility and functionality they bring. Not only do they benefit our health, they keep us feeling young, playful and confident. Start moving as much as possible throughout the day – walk in your lunch break, take the stairs rather than the lift when you're out shopping, and stretch or change position regularly when you're working at the computer. Try some fun movements – roll on the floor, balance on a safe kerb, climb a tree or go outside with your kids or some friends and play tag. Get creative and move more in whatever environment you find yourself in, whether that's your office, a park, your house or the gym.

IF YOU LEARN

FROM DEFEAT,

YOU HAVEN'T

REALLY LOST.

ZIG ZIGLAR

**Knowledge is limited.
Imagination encircles
the world.**

Albert Einstein

The Power of Song

Singing is good for your body and soul. Whether you sing in the shower or warble your way through karaoke, singing floods our bodies with feel-good endorphins and can boost our confidence and self-esteem. There are serious health benefits too. Singing has been linked to an improved immune system, larger lung capacity and longer life expectancy. Singing with others seems to have extra benefits. Researchers have discovered that choristers' heartbeats synchronize when they sing together, resulting in a calming effect that is as beneficial to their health as yoga. If singing in a group appeals, consider joining a choir, attending your local church, or starting an informal a capella group with some friends. Whether you sing in a group or in the privacy of your home or car, singing will never fail to uplift you.

AS LONG AS THE MIND
CAN ENVISION THE
FACT THAT YOU CAN
DO SOMETHING,
YOU CAN DO IT.

Arnold Schwarzenegger

Our life is what our thoughts make it.

Marcus Aurelius

CHILDLIKE JOY

Children are experts at having fun. They have the ability to see silliness and humour in everyday things such as a trip to the shops or a walk in the woods. To learn from children, watch how freely they play. Observe how they laugh out loud and throw themselves into creative projects, such as building a sandcastle or colouring in, with great enthusiasm. Make a point of carrying their exuberant spirit with you throughout the day. Start doing things for pure enjoyment. Take time to laugh, play, dance and sing. By adopting the carefree nature of your own children, your nieces and nephews, or even the kids you see playing in the park, you can bring more joy to your life and greet each day with a smile.

It's the simple things in life that are the most extraordinary; only wise men are able to understand them.

Paulo Coelho

Happiness consists not in having much, but in being content with little.

Marguerite Gardiner

Write a Haiku

In essence, a haiku is a short poem of three lines. It's a great way to jump in to creative writing as there are no strict rules and it's a far less daunting prospect than writing a short story or novel. You can write a haiku in seconds. It doesn't have to rhyme and you can write about anything – the weather, your cup of tea, or the view you see from your window. Pick your topic and let the words come to you. In order to release your inner poet,

avoid over-thinking and over-planning.
The aim is to use just a few words
to capture a moment and create a
picture in the reader's mind. Here's
an example of a traditional Japanese
haiku to get you started:

An old silent pond
A frog jumps into the pond
splash! Silence again

ONLY WHEN HE NO
LONGER KNOWS
WHAT HE IS DOING
DOES THE PAINTER
DO GOOD THINGS.

Edgar Degas

WHO ARE YOUR HEROES?

The world is filled with inspiring people who have overcome incredible odds to survive and thrive. Whatever your situation – whether you struggle with relationships, money or health – there will be someone out there who has experienced the same issue and can offer you hope, encouragement and wisdom. Seek out their stories, read their autobiographies, or watch documentaries and interviews, letting their words uplift and inspire you.

Make a Difference

Is there a cause or charity that is particularly important to you? Consider supporting an organization that is making a difference in this area. You can donate financially or with your time by volunteering. Joining an organization or subscribing to their newsletter will ensure you receive regular updates on their work and ways you can get involved. Even helping out with the smallest tasks can make a real difference to those in need of help. Contact volunteer centres for opportunities and advice, as well as websites such as www.do-it.org. You can also approach community projects directly – theatres, museums, libraries, animal shelters, youth organizations and conservation groups are likely to welcome an extra pair of hands. Voluntary work is a great way to learn new skills, meet new people and find a new sense of meaning and purpose in your life.

WE CAN DO
ANYTHING WE
WANT TO DO IF
WE STICK TO IT
LONG ENOUGH.

HELEN KELLER

It is always the simple that produces the marvellous.

Amelia Barr

BEYOND THE BRUSH

To stimulate your creativity, put down your pens and pencils and use unusual materials to create a work of art. There are all sorts of objects around the house and in nature that can be used to create interesting marks. You could dip a twig or feather into ink, or press a piece of bubble wrap into wet paint and see what marks they create, for example. Or use petals and sweet wrappers to make a colourful collage. Alternatively, go back to being a kid again and just use your hands.

Creating art using unfamiliar materials can help you break out of your comfort zone and move past the rules and routines that may have limited you in the past. It can encourage you to try new things and reconnect with your originality and playfulness, which can have a positive impact on all areas of your life.

YOU CAN BREAK
THAT BIG PLAN INTO
SMALL STEPS AND
TAKE THE FIRST STEP
RIGHT AWAY.

Indira Gandhi

**Regret for wasted time
is more wasted time.**

Mason Cooley

Buddy Up

Do you know a friend or colleague who wants to set a self-improvement goal or accomplish a dream? If so, consider joining them in a buddy system. Being accountable to a "buddy" is one of the best ways to make sure you don't get distracted from your goals. By meeting regularly – weekly or monthly – you can check each other's progress, offer words of encouragement and, of course, celebrate your achievements. Whether you have a yoga buddy writing buddy or business buddy, they need to be reliable, supportive and committed, so choose your buddy carefully. Teaming up with the right partner can dramatically increase your chances of success

Do not worry about your originality. You could not get rid of it even if you wanted to.

Robert Henri

PEOPLE POWER

It's said that we are the average of the five people we spend the most time with. Take an honest look at your business and social life. Do you spend time with negative people who drain you and sap your spirit? If possible, limit your contact with these people and seek the company of happy, optimistic and successful people who will inspire you to achieve your full potential.

Mind-wandering

You may think daydreaming is a waste of time, but in fact it's a crucial part of the creative process. Your brain is not wired to be focused in a straight line all the time. Allowing your mind to wander at will can boost creativity and imagination, and even inspire great works of art and science. J. K. Rowling credits daydreaming with her best ideas. Arthur Fry came up for the idea for Post-It notes when he was daydreaming in church and Albert Einstein came up with his theory of relativity while imagining himself riding a sunbeam to the edge of the universe. Take regular breaks throughout the day and grab moments of "down time" whenever you can, such as on a train journey or while waiting in a queue. From now on, don't feel guilty if your thoughts start to wander – it could be the catalyst for your next big idea.

Go confidently in the direction of your dreams. Live the life you have imagined.

Henry David Thoreau

The muse visits during the act of creation, not before.

Roger Ebert

DON'T COMPLAIN

A simple way to transform your life
is to stop complaining. Give it a go.
Commit to one day of zero gossiping,
criticizing and complaining. You'll
soon realize what a great habit this is.
We complain about the weather, the
traffic, our jobs and other people. The
problem is, the more we complain, the
unhappier we become. This is because
our brains notice more of whatever we
focus on. So, if you spend your days
whinging and moaning, you'll always
find plenty of things to complain

about. Start to notice whenever you feel the temptation to make a negative comment. Some people swear by wearing a rubber band around their wrist and snapping it or switching it to the other wrist whenever they realize their thoughts have turned negative. This works as a pattern breaker – it gets your attention and brings you back to the present moment. Another trick is to simply ask yourself when you open your mouth: "Would I rather complain or be happy?" Commit to one complaint-free day and see how much better you feel.

OBSTACLES ARE THOSE FRIGHTFUL THINGS YOU SEE WHEN YOU TAKE YOUR EYES OFF YOUR GOAL.

HENRY FORD

Your mind will answer most questions if you learn to relax and wait for the answer.

William S. Burroughs

GO OUTSIDE

Sometimes all we need to get back on track is to spend time outdoors. When we're at one with nature, our minds can relax and our senses are reinvigorated. Take a walk in the woods, sit by a river, or lie down in the grass and feel the earth beneath you. Switch off your phone and take in the sights, sounds and scents of nature.

Life is like photography; we develop from the negatives.

Anonymous

Rest is Best

Sleep is a crucial foundation of overall health, well-being and inspiration. Good-quality sleep gives you the essential energy you need to be creative in your waking hours. And your dreams may even provide you with ideas you can turn into reality, whether it's the inspiration for an abstract painting, a fantasy novel or a business venture.

It's tempting to think that staying up late and working longer makes you more productive, but it's more likely to drain you of your creative sharpness. Try going to bed earlier and making a fresh start in the morning. Your brain and body will feel refreshed after a good night's slumber, allowing you to make progress on your chosen project before the day has a chance to wear you out. Give it a go – even if you're more of a night owl than an early bird – and seize the day sooner.

IF YOU THINK YOU
ARE TOO SMALL TO
MAKE A DIFFERENCE,
TRY SLEEPING WITH
A MOSQUITO.

Dalai Lama

I am seeking. I am striving. I am in it with all my heart.

Vincent Van Gogh

ASK SOMEONE HAPPY

The happiness and enthusiasm of others can be infectious. Spend time with people who possess these qualities. Ask them to tell you about the things they love most in life and watch their faces light up as they share their passions. You could even ask them what they consider to be the most important lesson they've ever learned. By listening to their words of joy and wisdom, you'll learn valuable information that you can apply to your own life.

THE IMPORTANT
THING... IS NOT HOW
MANY YEARS IN YOUR
LIFE, BUT HOW MUCH
LIFE IN YOUR YEARS!

Edward J. Stieglitz

A Quote a Day

Do you have a favourite quote or saying that has got you through a hard time or inspired you to achieve a dream? Place your favourite motivational words where you can see them every day – perhaps print them out and stick them to your bathroom mirror or computer screen, or carry them with you in your bag or wallet.

Surround yourself with positive thoughts, advice and ideas from the world's greatest thinkers, both past and present. Browse inspirational quotes on websites such as www. tinybuddha.com and consider buying a small book of quotes to keep by your bedside. You might even find a new favourite within the pages of this book. Dip into these sources of wisdom on a regular basis and highlight your favourite feel-good words. The right quote can shift your mindset and turn your whole day around in a second.

I don't measure a man's success by how high he climbs but how high he bounces when he hits bottom.

George S. Patton

Only those
who will
risk going
too far can
possibly
find out
how far
one can go.

T. S. Eliot

TAKE SOME CREDIT

When life feels like an uphill struggle, focus on how far you've come, as opposed to the distance still to go. If you're running a new business, for example, instead of seeing your imperfect website and all the ideas and strategies you've yet to implement, acknowledge all the progress you have made to get to this point. Give yourself credit for your hard work and perseverance. You may not be exactly where you'd like to be, but you've come a long way. Try writing a list of your accomplishments over the last year or two. Include progress in your self-knowledge, relationships, spirituality, health and career. Then look at your list and reflect on just how much you've achieved. Focusing exclusively on all the things you have left to do can rob you of joy and pride in your accomplishments, so from now on, celebrate how far you have come and marvel at how much your life has changed for the better.

THE WORLD IS BUT
A CANVAS TO OUR
IMAGINATION.

HENRY DAVID THOREAU

First say to yourself what you would be; and then do what you have to do.

Epictetus

Dream it.
Believe it.

Achieve it.

If you're interested in finding
out more about our books,
find us on Facebook at
Summersdale Publishers
and follow us on Twitter
at **@Summersdale**.

www.summersdale.com

Image credits